ideals® FRIENDSHIP

More Than 50 Years of Celebrating Life's Most Treasured Moments

Vol. 55, No. 4

"Of all the means to ensure happiness throughout the whole of life, by far the most important is the acquisition of friends"

—*Epicurus*

IDEALS—Vol. 55, No. 4 July MCMXCVIII IDEALS (ISSN 0019-137X) is published six times a year: January, March, May, July, September, and November by IDEALS PUBLICATIONS INCORPORATED, 535 Metroplex Drive, Suite 250, Nashville, TN 37211. Periodical postage paid at Nashville, Tennessee, and additional mailing offices. Copyright © MCMXCVIII by IDEALS PUBLICATIONS INCORPORATED. POSTMASTER: Send address changes to Ideals, PO Box 305300, Nashville, TN 37230. All rights reserved. Title IDEALS registered U.S. Patent Office.

SINGLE ISSUE—U.S. $5.95 USD; Higher in Canada
ONE-YEAR SUBSCRIPTION—U.S. $19.95 USD; Canada $36.00 CDN (incl. GST and shipping); Foreign $25.95 USD
TWO-YEAR SUBSCRIPTION—U.S. $35.95 USD; Canada $66.50 CDN (incl. GST and shipping); Foreign $47.95 USD

Subscribers may call customer service at 1-800-558-4343 to make address changes. Unsolicited manuscripts will not be returned without a self-addressed, stamped envelope.

ISBN 0-8249-1150-4 GST 131903775

Cover Photo
A SUNNY DAY BOUQUET
H. Armstrong Roberts

Inside Front Cover
WALKING IN THE HILLS
Edward Henry Potthast, artist
Christie's Images

Inside Back Cover
THE VISITOR
Arthur Hopkins, artist
Christie's Images

A Summer Ramble

The quiet August noon has come;
 A slumbrous silence fills the sky.
The fields are still, the woods are dumb;
 In glassy sleep the water lies.

Away! I will not be, today,
 The only slave of toil and care;
Away from desk and dust! Away!
 I'll be as idle as the air.

Beneath the open sky abroad,
 Among the plants and breathing things,
The sinless, peaceful works of God,
 I'll share the calm the season brings.

Come, thou, in whose soft eyes I see
 The gentle meaning of thy heart,
One day amid the woods with me,
 From men and all their cares apart.

William Cullen Bryant

Horses graze near Vida, Oregon. Photograph by Dick Dietrich.

SONG OF THE BROOK

I come from haunts of coot and hern,
    I make a sudden sally
And sparkle out among the fern
    To bicker down a valley.

By thirty hills I hurry down
    Or slip between the ridges,
By twenty thorps, a little town,
    And half a hundred bridges.

Till last by Philip's farm I flow
    To join the brimming river.
For men may come and men may go,
    But I go on forever.

I chatter over stony ways
    In little sharps and trebles;
I bubble into eddying bays,
    I babble on the pebbles.

With many a curve my banks I fret
    By many a field and fallow
And many a fairy foreland set
    With willow-weed and mallow.

I chatter, chatter, as I flow
    To join the brimming river.
For men may come and men may go,
    But I go on forever.

I wind about, and in and out,
    With here a blossom sailing,

With here and there a lusty trout,
    And here and there a grayling,

And here and there a foamy flake
    Upon me, as I travel
With many a silvery waterbreak
    Above the golden gravel

And draw them all along and flow
    To join the brimming river.
For men may come and men may go,
    But I go on forever.

I steal by lawns and grassy plots,
    I slide by hazel covers;
I move the sweet forget-me-nots
    That grow for happy lovers.

I slip, I slide, I gloom, I glance
    Among my skimming swallows;
I make the netted sunbeam dance
    Against my shady shallows.

I murmur under moon and stars
    In brambly wildernesses;
I linger by my shingly bars,
    I loiter round my cresses

And out again I curve and flow
    To join the brimming river.
For men may come and men may go,
    But I go on forever.

Alfred, Lord Tennyson

Cottonwood trees along the Virgin River decorate the Gateway to the Narrows in Zion National Park, Utah. Photograph by Terry Donnelly.

THE IDLE LIFE I LEAD

The idle life I lead
Is like a pleasant sleep,
Wherein I rest and heed
The dreams that by me sweep.

And still of all my dreams
In turn so swiftly past,
Each in its fancy seems
A nobler than the last.

And every eve I say,
Noting my step in bliss,
That I have known no day
In all my life like this.

Robert Bridges

REST

Rest is not quitting
The busy career,
Rest is the fitting
Of self to its sphere.

'Tis the brook's motion,
Clear without strife,
Fleeing to ocean
After its life.

'Tis loving and serving
The Highest and Best!
'Tis onwards, unswerving;
And that is true rest.

John Sullivan Dwight

Early Autumn colors the foliage surrounding the Moon Bridge in the Japanese Garden in Portland, Oregon. Photograph by Jon Gnass/Jon Gnass Photo Images.

TREE AT MY WINDOW

Tree at my window, window tree,
My sash is lowered when night comes on;
But let there never be curtain drawn
Between you and me.

Vague dream-head lifted out of the ground,
And thing next most diffuse to cloud,
Not all your light tongues talking aloud
Could be profound.

But tree, I have seen you taken and tossed,
And if you have seen me when I slept,
You have seen me when I was taken and swept
And all but lost.

That day she put our heads together,
Fate had her imagination about her,
Your head so much concerned with outer,
Mine with inner, weather.

Robert Frost

*Fall-colored ivy and a blooming window box frame a curtained window
in Iowa County, Wisconsin. Photograph by Terry Donnelly.*

Autumn Pastoral

Like old men smacking dry lips over cider
The leaves are tasting autumn in the air;
And in low valleys where the hills stretch wider,
The smell of woodsmoke spirals slow and clear.
Thin orchards yawn into the wind, their fruit
Spent swiftly as the years have dropped away;
And in the dangling silence a lone bee's lute
Stitches a yellow seam across the day.
Where sumac ripens redder in the sun
And goldenrod drifts pale, reluctant dust,
Two lovers rise and walk the fields as one,
Pledging eternal love with eager eyes,
Blind to the swift year turning now to rust,
The wild geese thundering south through blackening skies.

Daniel Whitehead Hicky

The Wisconsin River Valley swings into fall harvest as seen from the Gibralter Rock State Natural Area in Sauk County, Wisconsin. Photograph by Mary Liz Austin.

A brilliant afternoon in early autumn finds the Red Mountain Pass between Silverton and Ouray, Colorado,

a peaceful idyll of welcome respite for travelers through the wilderness. Photograph by Dick Dietrich.

YELLOW FLOWERS

The painted-cups, the pitcher-plants,
The rock-set columbines that dance
With every breeze, the gentian's blue,
Joy Pye weed's lovely, old rose hue,
The bloodroot, the anemone—
Each carries thoughts of God to me.

But somehow in the *golden* things
Each season prodigally brings,
I find Him most to meet my need.
The cowslip and the jewel-weed,
The buttercup, wood betony—
Each brings Him very near to me.

Who has not felt his throat grow tense
When on some zigzag country fence
He glimpses trailing bittersweet?
Who has not walked with reverent feet
Through paths made bright by goldenrod,
And breathed a voiceless "Thank you, God"?

Bertha Gerneaux Woods

*Purple loosestrife and goldenrod highlight a roadside in Merrimack,
New Hampshire. Photograph by William Johnson/Johnson's Photography.*

The Light of a New Day

I watched the sun come to my place the other morning. It started from a hill a half-mile south of me. The hill slopes into a tree-shaded valley before the road starts climbing again toward the knoll where I live.

Only the hill was bathed in light when the sun first appeared over the eastern horizon. Because of the shade of the woodland trees on this side of the hill, the sun seemed to dally on its way with no hurried purpose at all.

The morning was bright and cool and clear. Dew had formed on the goldenrod and the purple morning-glories and on the pastures and fields that bordered the roadside. It was an ideal morning for the sun to mark the beginning of a new day, sparkling and fresh, the light reaching down to touch a land rested by the coolness of night.

The sun moved on slowly toward my homeplace as fingers of light alternated with those of the shadows as they pointed to the green meadows along the way. As the sun climbed higher, its light swept away more and more of the shadows of the trees. The tree-tops gleamed in red, scarlet, and gold.

Finally, the sun arrived. There were still shadows of buildings and dooryard trees. But these were morning shadows, unlike those of later afternoon, those quiet shadows, dark and deep and serene.

There that morning I watched the coming of a new day, young and fresh and strong. Born of the dawn that brought those sparkling and gleaming rays of the morning sun. I stood waiting. I wanted the soothing touch upon my face, soothing as the warmth of a cheek pressed to mine.

The author of two published books, Lansing Christman has been con-tributing to Ideals for more than twenty years. Mr. Christman has also been published in several American, foreign, and braille antholo-gies. He lives in rural South Carolina.

Sunrise washes the landscape of the Great Smoky Mountains National Park in Tennessee. Photograph by William Johnson/Johnson's Photography.

Beautiful color in this backyard garden charms visitors to this home on Vashon Island, Washington. Photograph by Terry Donnelly.

Friendship

Friendship is a common home-grown flower,
But most uncommon are its growing ways—
Its seed can quicken, root within an hour,
Its lovely bloom survive the wintriest days.
It bears transplanting best when fully grown
With roots fine-tendriled, spreading wide and deep;
Removed, it lives on memory-soil alone—
A phantom field where death-winds ever sweep.
It is refreshed by fountains long gone dry,
This everlasting flower that will not die.

Sudie Stuart Hager

From My Garden Journal

by Deana Deck

POPPY

*"In Flanders Fields the poppies blow
Between the crosses, row on row . . ."*
—John McCrae

McCrae's poem was written in 1915 in honor of the thousands of young American men who died on foreign soil during the first World War. When I was in grade school, my grandfather gave me a small, red crepe paper flower to pin on my dress on Armistice Day. That was my first introduction to the flower known as the poppy. It became a vivid reminder of that event for an entire generation, which may explain why the flower gradually declined in popularity as first-hand memories of the "Great War" faded.

For years I associated the poppy with the holiday and thought of it as a symbol rather than as a real plant. The first blooming poppies I ever saw weren't even red; they were yellow. We lived in California at the time, so it's not so unusual that the plants were the native California Poppy, the official state flower. Although this was the poppy I thought of when I ate a poppy-seed roll, the California poppy is not a member of the vast *Papaver* family, the source of those tiny, crispy poppy seeds.

The poppy's decline in popularity might have been because of its color. The bright red poppy used to be one of the few varieties available, but the red of the poppy is so vivid it nearly glows and can be overpowering in large plantings. A grouping of just three plants will rivet attention to themselves and deliver a blast of color with which few plants outside of the zinnia can compete.

Most people prefer more subtle colors in their gardens. Recently, hybridizers have developed cultivars of the poppy in an ever-increasing array of pastels. As a result, poppies have become immensely popular once more. The genus *Papaver* includes about ninety species, most of them native to temperate and subtropical regions of the world.

The petals of the poppy resemble soft, colorful ruffles of crepe paper—a good choice of materials for creating artificial poppies. The small lapel flower—still sold to honor all war veterans—can't hold a candle to the real poppy with its immense four- to six-inch blooms of gorgeous intense color.

Poppy blooms are carried on tall stalks that can reach two feet in height, which makes a dramatic statement in the garden. The foliage consists of either toothed, lobed, or thick fern-like basal leaves that form a nest-like rosette near the ground. The hairy-looking flower stalks grow up out of this nest of greenery, and each stalk bears a single bloom. In mid-spring the plants bloom profusely. As the heat of sum-

POPPY

mer comes, however, leaves and all, move into a dormancy that will last until fall. Once the weather begins to cool, the basal leaves reappear and can survive even in the worst winter weather, often under snow.

The Oriental (*Papaver orientale*) poppy is one of the most familiar. A perennial from the Middle East, the Oriental produces red, pink, or white flowers as large as six inches across. Although the classic red version is the most widely available, there are some other lovely varieties, among them the Degas. Think of the pink tutus worn by the ballerinas in Edgar Degas' paintings and you'll have a fairly accurate idea of the soft, salmon-pink color of the Degas poppy. Another unusual color available is the Raspberry Queen, which is a lovely raspberry sherbet color.

One poppy often sold as a perennial, but which is really a half-hardy annual in most of the United States, is the *Papaver nudicaule*. This plant is listed as the Iceland poppy, but garden catalogs also call it the Australian poppy. It grows from the Arctic regions southward to Colorado. It's a difficult poppy to grow because it won't tolerate hot weather. It can be grown in winter and early spring in California, the warm southwestern states, and in the deep South.

Because perennial poppies can't tolerate heat and bloom too early in mild winters (making them highly vulnerable to the occasional late frost), annual varieties are better for gardens in warmer climates. Annual poppies, however, do have a longer blooming season than the perennials. One relatively small-bloomed annual species is *Papaver rhoeas*, the Flanders poppy now sold mostly as the corn poppy. It grows wild along the northwestern coast of what used to be Flanders and is now part of Belgium. Its flowers are red, scarlet, deep purple, or white.

Another annual variety, the one from which seeds are obtained for those tasty poppy seed rolls and muffins, is *Papaver somniferum*. A native of Greece and the Orient, the flowers are often double, in white, pink, red, or purple, with three- to four-inch wide blooms.

Poppies are relatively carefree plants, suffering few insect or disease problems. The one thing they require, in addition to full sun, is soil that drains quickly. This is especially important in winter, because the long tap root of the dormant plant will rot in wet soil. Annual poppies require the same conditions; and although the seeds like damp soil when germinating, once the plant forms leaves it prefers drier conditions. Annual seeds can be planted as early as late January in the south, and late February or early March in more northern climates. Because the seeds are so tiny, it's easier to plant them if you mix them with a handful of sand and sprinkle the sand into the bed.

Because poppies bloom in the late spring and early summer and go dormant very early, combining them with companion plantings helps disguise the bare spots they'll leave behind. Coreopsis, rudebeckia, Russian sage, and red Penstemon are good choices. These plants tend to bloom at about the same time that the poppies are dying back.

One nice reminder that the poppy leaves behind when it becomes dormant is the attractive seed pod. These are easily dried and add dramatic interest to flower arrangements. You don't have to plant many poppies to obtain the seed pods, and you only have to open one ripe pod to obtain enough seeds for a garden full of blooms. That makes it easy to share poppies—flowers, pods, or seeds—with your friends!

Deana Deck tends her flowers, plants, and vegetables at her home in Nashville, Tennessee, where her popular garden column is a regular feature in The Tennessean.

THE HOUSE
BY THE SIDE
OF THE ROAD

There are hermit souls that live withdrawn
    In the place of their self-content;
There are souls like stars that dwell apart
    In a fellowless firmament;
There are pioneer souls that blaze their paths
    Where highways never ran—
But let me live by the side of the road
    And be a friend to man.

Let me live in a house by the side of the road
    Where the race of men go by—
The men who are good and the men who are bad,
    As good and as bad as I.
I would not sit in the scorner's seat
    Or hurl the cynic's ban—
Let me live in a house by the side of the road
    And be a friend to man.

I see from my house by the side of the road,
    By the side of the highway of life,
The men who press with the ardor of hope,
    The men who are faint with the strife;
But I turn not away from their smiles nor their tears,
    Both parts of an infinite plan—
Let me live in a house by the side of the road
    And be a friend to man.

I know there are brook-gladdened meadows ahead,
    And mountains of wearisome height;
That the road passes on through the long afternoon
    And stretches away to the night.
And still I rejoice when the travelers rejoice
    And weep with the strangers that moan,
Nor live in my house by the side of the road
    Like a man who dwells alone.

Let me live in my house by the side of the road,
    Where the race of men go by—
They are good, they are bad, they are weak, they are strong,
    Wise, foolish—so am I.
Then why should I sit in the scorner's seat,
    Or hurl the cynic's ban?
Let me live in my house by the side of the road
    And be a friend to man.

Sam Walter Foss

*Autumn leaves dot the walkway to the Ford Mansion in the
Morristown National Historical Park, New Jersey. Photograph by Jess Gnass.*

FORBEARANCE

Hast thou named all the birds without a gun?
Loved the wood-rose, and left it on its stalk?
At rich men's tables eaten bread and pulse?
Unarmed, faced danger with a heart of trust?
And loved so well a high behavior,
In man or maid, that thou from speech refrained,
Nobility more nobly to repay?
O be my friend and teach me to be thine!

Ralph Waldo Emerson

Cultivate forbearance till your heart yields a fine crop of it. Pray for a short memory as to all unkindnesses.

Charles Spurgeon

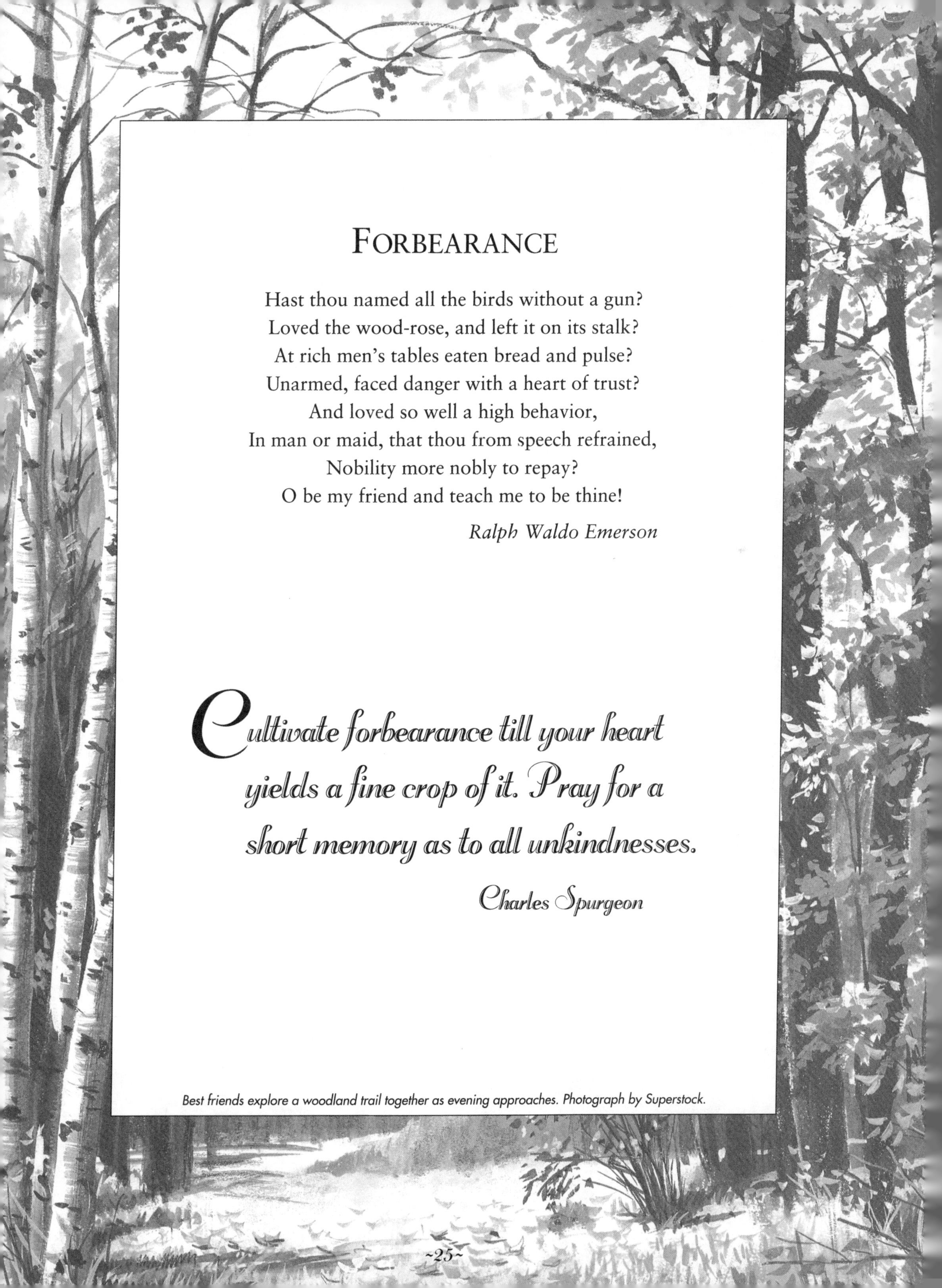

Best friends explore a woodland trail together as evening approaches. Photograph by Superstock.

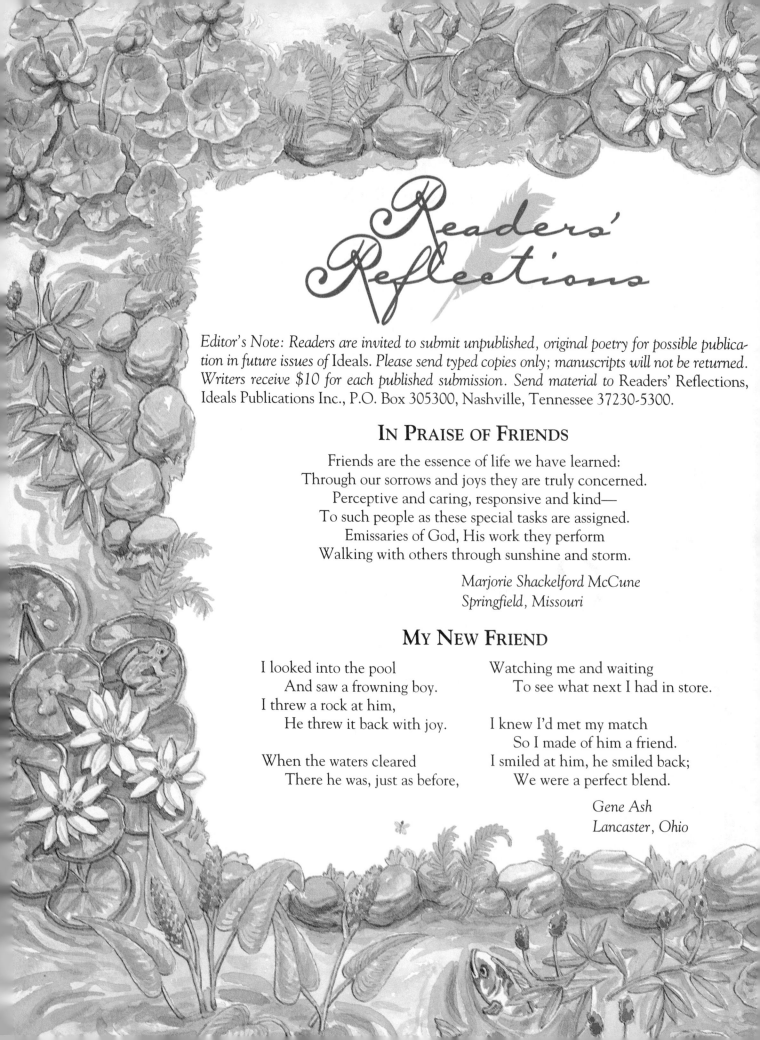

Readers' Reflections

Editor's Note: Readers are invited to submit unpublished, original poetry for possible publication in future issues of Ideals. *Please send typed copies only; manuscripts will not be returned. Writers receive $10 for each published submission. Send material to Readers' Reflections, Ideals Publications Inc., P.O. Box 305300, Nashville, Tennessee 37230-5300.*

IN PRAISE OF FRIENDS

Friends are the essence of life we have learned:
Through our sorrows and joys they are truly concerned.
Perceptive and caring, responsive and kind—
To such people as these special tasks are assigned.
Emissaries of God, His work they perform
Walking with others through sunshine and storm.

Marjorie Shackelford McCune
Springfield, Missouri

MY NEW FRIEND

I looked into the pool
    And saw a frowning boy.
I threw a rock at him,
    He threw it back with joy.

When the waters cleared
    There he was, just as before,

Watching me and waiting
    To see what next I had in store.

I knew I'd met my match
    So I made of him a friend.
I smiled at him, he smiled back;
    We were a perfect blend.

Gene Ash
Lancaster, Ohio

AUTUMN'S ARRIVAL

I saw two yellow leaves today;
    While all around was green—
It meant that autumn had arrived
    Though it hardly could be seen.

I saw two yellow leaves today;
    The sky was bright and blue—
And yet I knew they meant for us
    That fall had come anew.

I saw two yellow leaves today;
    That dangled from a tree—
But since I love the autumn so,
    They meant a lot to me!

Hope C. Oberhelman
Lubbock, Texas

FAREWELL, GREEN FIELDS

Farewell, green fields of summer,
    The splendor of the grass,
Flecked with colors dancing,
    Along remote, untrodden paths.

Farewell, wild crimson roses,
    Deflowered by the wind,
Lush petals crowned with glory,
    Now waxing pale and spectre-thin.

Farewell, my rustic countryside,
    Tranquil haven of repose,
Until the fields are emerald green,
    And the bloom is on the rose.

Barbara Cagle Ray
Nashville, Tennessee

FRIENDSHIP

Friendship is like a garden
    With different flowers everywhere;
Some are your very favorites
    And you treat them with tender care.

Others may drift by the wayside
    They soon wither and fade away;
But some will continue to blossom
    In true "friendship" day after day.

And I pray in my life's garden
    I've planted friendships to keep;

That I have sowed some kindness
    And I've planted it good and deep.

And as I count my blessings
    And my flowers one by one;
I see your face among them
    Glowing in the morning sun.

God's helped me with my garden
    He's been there my whole life through;
And He gave me the greatest gift
    When He gave me a friend like you.

Lola Moore
Coldwater, Michigan

Frolic

The children were shouting together
   And racing along the sands,
A glimmer of dancing shadows,
   A dovelike flutter of hands.

The stars were shouting in heaven,
   The sun was chasing the moon:
The game was the same as the children's,
   They danced to the self-same tune.

The whole of the world was merry,
   One joy from the vale to the height,
Where the blue woods of twilight encircled
   The lovely lawns of the light.

AE (George William Russell)

White Butterflies

Fly, white butterflies, out to sea,
Frail, pale wings for the wind to try,
Small white wings that we scarce can see,
   Fly!

Some fly light as a laugh of glee,
Some fly soft as a long, low sigh;
All to the haven where each would be,
   Fly!

Algernon Charles Swinburne

Artist Edward Henry Potthast depicts the carefree exuberance
of a day at the seashore in Children on the Beach.
Image from Hirshorn Museum, Washington D.C./Superstock.

VALUED FAMILY FRIENDS

The children had pets of their own, too, of course. Among them guinea-pigs were the stand-bys—their highly unemotional nature fits them for companionship with adoring but overenthusiastic young masters and mistresses. Then there were flying squirrels, and kangaroo-rats, gentle and trustful, and a badger whose temper was short but whose nature was fundamentally friendly. The badger's name was Josiah; the particular little boy whose property he was used to carry him about, clasped firmly around what would have been his waist if he had had any. Inasmuch as when on the ground the badger would play energetic games of tag with the little boy and nip his bare legs, I suggested that it would be uncommonly disagreeable if he took advantage of being held in the little boy's arms to bite his face; but this suggestion was repelled with scorn as an unworthy assault on the character of Josiah. 'He bites legs sometimes, but he never bites faces,' said the little boy. We also had a young black bear whom the children christened Jonathan Edwards, partly out of compliment to their mother, who was descended from that great Puritan divine, and partly because the bear possessed a temper in which gloom and strength were combined in what the children regarded as Calvinistic proportions. As for the dogs, of course there were many, and during their lives they were intimate and valued family friends, and their deaths were household tragedies. One of them, a large yellow animal of several good breeds and valuable rather because of psychical than physical traits, was named 'Susan' by his small owners, in commemoration of another retainer, a white cow; the fact that the cow and the dog were not of the same sex being treated with indifference.

Theodore Roosevelt
from An Autobiography

A little girl whispers secrets to her pet guinea pig. Photograph by J. Nettis/H. Armstrong Roberts.
Mother's knitting basket offers a comfortable bed to a tiny kitten. Photograph by Dick Dietrich.
A puppy finds comfort in his young owner's arms. Photograph by Todd Langley/Uniphoto.

FOR THE CHILDREN

END-OF-SUMMER POEM

The little songs of summer
Are all gone today.
The little insect instruments
Are all packed away:
The bumblebee's snare drum,
The grasshopper's guitar,
The katydid's castanets—
I wonder where they are.
The bullfrog's banjo,
The cricket's violin,
The dragonfly's cello
Have ceased their merry din.
Oh, where is the orchestra?
From harpist down to drummer
They've all disappeared
With the passing of the summer.

Rowena Bastin Bennett

American artist Donald Zolan captures the disappointment of a canceled ball game in Rained Out. © Zolan Fine Arts, Ltd. Hershey, Pennsylvania.

A Lesson from Childhood

One time, investigating in the backyard of our house in Temuco the tiny objects and minuscule beings of my world, I came upon a hole in one of the boards of the fence. I looked through the hole and saw a landscape like that behind our house, uncared for and wild. I moved back a few steps, because I sensed vaguely that something was about to happen. All of a sudden a hand appeared—a tiny hand of a boy about my own age. By the time I came close again, the hand was gone, and in its place there was a marvellous white sheep.

The sheep's wool was faded. Its wheels had escaped. All of this only made it more authentic. I had never seen such a wonderful sheep. I looked back through the hole but the boy had disappeared. I went into the house and brought out a treasure of my own: a pine cone, opened, full of odor and resin, which I adored. I set it down in the same spot and went off with the sheep.

I never saw either the hand or the boy again. And I have never again seen a sheep like that either. The toy I lost finally in a fire. But even now, in 1954, almost fifty years old, whenever I pass a toyshop, I look furtively into the window, but it's no use. They don't make sheep like that any more.

I have been a lucky man. To feel the intimacy of brothers is a marvelous thing in life. To feel the love of people whom we love is a fire that feeds our life. But to feel the affection that comes from those whom we do not know, from those unknown to us, who are watching over our sleep and solitude, over our dangers and our weaknesses—that is something still greater and more beautiful because it widens out the boundaries of our being, and unites all living things.

That exchange brought home to me for the first time a precious idea: that all of humanity is somehow together. That experience came to me again much later; this time it stood out strikingly against a background of trouble and persecution.

It won't surprise you then that I attempted to give something resiny, earthlike, and fragrant in exchange for human brotherhood. Just as I once left the pine cone by the fence, I have since left my words on the door of so many people who were unknown to me, people in prison, or hunted, or alone.

That is the great lesson I learned in my childhood, in the backyard of a lonely house. Maybe it was nothing but a game two boys played who didn't know each other and wanted to pass to the other some good things of life. Yet maybe this small and mysterious exchange of gifts remained inside me also, deep and indestructible, giving my poetry light.

Pablo Neruda
from Childhood and Poetry

Wildflowers accent a backyard fence in LaSalle County, Illinois. Photograph by Terry Donnelly.

The Boys

Where are they—the friends of my childhood enchanted?
The clear, laughing eyes looking back in my own
And the warm, chubby fingers my palms have so wanted,
As when we raced over pink pastures of clover
And mocked the quail's whir and the bumblebee's drone?

Have the breezes of time blown their blossomy faces
Forever adrift down the years that are flown?
Am I never to see them romp back to their places,
      Where over the meadow,
      In sunshine and shadow,
The meadow-larks trill and the bumblebees drone?
Where are they? Ah, dim in the dust lies the clover;
The whippoorwill's call has a sorrowful tone,
And the dove's—I have wept at it over and over.
I want the glad lustre of youth and the cluster
Of faces asleep where the bumblebees drone!

James Whitcomb Riley

*Artist Lauritz Andersen Ring portrays the quiet serenity of an evening walk
in Old Man Walking in a Rye Field. Image from Christie's Images/Superstock.*

Three Friends

Of all the blessings which my life has known,
I value most and most praise God for three:
Want, Loneliness, and Pain, those comrades true,
Who masqueraded in the garb of foes
For many a year and filled my heart with dread.
Yet fickle joys, like false, pretentious friends,
Have proved less worthy than this trio. First,
Want taught me labor, led me up the steep
And toilsome paths to hills of pure delight,
Trod only by the feet that know fatigue,
And yet press on until the heights appear.
Then loneliness and hunger of the heart
Sent me upreaching to the realms of space,
Till all the silences grew eloquent,
And all their loving forces hailed me friend.
Last, pain taught prayer! placed in my hand the staff
Of close communion with my humble soul,
That I might lean upon it to the end
And find myself made strong for any strife.
And then these three who had pursued my steps
Like stern, relentless foes, year after year,
Unmasked, and turned their faces full on me
And lo! they were divinely beautiful,
For through them shone the lustrous eyes of Love.

Ella Wheeler Wilcox

Nostalgic treasures gathered from Grandmother's attic provide a glimpse into yesteryear. Photograph by Jessie Walker.

THE KEYS TO FRIENDSHIP

On a day of rain and wind, I decided to poke around in the attic. An attic is a lovely and maddening place for everything is there that you do not know what in the world to do with. In a burst of enthusiasm for clearing it out, we sold five spinning wheels and a carder some years ago. But there are still old chests full of odds and ends, and that is exactly what they are. I do not mean to say Jill and I are hoarders. We are givers-away. Anything we do not wear inside of a year is given away because as Jill puts it, "If we didn't need that for a year, someone else does." But there are things like paintings and water colors that are rather old-fashioned. No doubt fifty years from now, they'll be collector's items. Meanwhile we do not know who would like them, so there they are. . . .

But the one thing that is a main problem is the keys. I cannot understand why we have so many old keys. They do not seem to fit anything, so far as we can find out. Some of them are very old, tiny, and delicate, some of them are big enough to lock a barn door. Since neither Jill nor I ever lock anything, we are at a loss to understand what these keys are for. A few of them have faded rose or lilac ribbons attached, so they must be important. Jill points out that since we never lock anything, why not just toss the whole box? And I always say that maybe we might need a key one day. Somehow a key has a fascination for me, except that I would not want to use one. A key is a mystery of a sort. It means something might be unlocked some time. . . .

When I was very young, I had a treasure box, made of metal which looked like gold, but wasn't. I kept the most important and cherished items in this, and kept the key in a spot where I hoped my father would not find it. When I opened it, a few years ago, I found all of youth in it. I found a dance program filled entirely with one name. I found a high school athletic letter, the football A. I found three sticks of gum tied with pink ribbon. I could *not* remember the significance of these. I found a few letters which really said nothing, and yet breathed of young love as arbutus breathes of spring. And I found a perfectly hideous silk handkerchief with San Antonio, Texas, painted on it. And when I repacked the box, and locked it, I did not even throw away the gum. Some day, I thought, I'll remember why that gum was given to me, and since I never chewed gum, I'll wonder whether I did chew one piece or not! . . .

As I took the box of keys back to the place under the eaves in the attic, I thought it a good idea that some secret places do have to have keys, for after all fitting a key into a lock is an act of faith. It means we believe the key will fit, the lock will accept it. And this, in itself, is a wonder. Also, conversely, we sense when a key will not fit.

There are times when just a few words unlock a friendship.

"I wanted to be friends, so much, but I just could not find the right words to say." I've heard this more than once. I have felt it myself when the magic key to friendship was not there. But then there are times when just a few words unlock a friendship. They are usually very simple words, not words trying to make an impression. But they unlock a door.

I come back down the ladder stairs thinking that I really should have thrown out those keys, along with a good many other things. But every now and then we go to the attic and find something we need, old hand-wrought hinges, a few black-oak hand-cut boards, old picture frames. And if the front door suddenly locks itself, Jill says, "I think there's a key in the attic that might fit."

Gladys Taber

BITS & PIECES

Old friends are best. King James used to call for his old shoes: they were easiest for his feet.

John Selden

Friendship is a miracle by which a person consents to view from a certain distance, and without coming any nearer, the very being who is necessary to him as food.

Simone Weil

To be capable of steady friendship or lasting love, are the two greatest proofs, not only of goodness of heart, but of strength of mind.

William Hazlitt

Your friend is your field which you sow with love and reap with thanksgiving.

Kahlil Gibran

Friendship . . . does not abolish distance between human beings but brings that distance to life.

Walter Benjamin

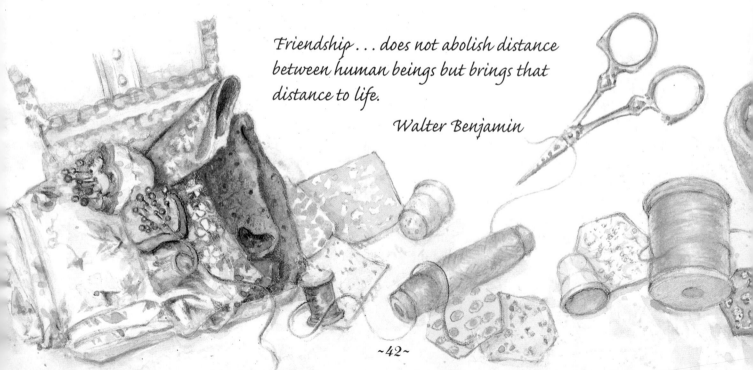

From quiet homes and first beginning, Out to the undis-
covered ends, There's nothing worth the wear of winning,
But laughter and the love of friends.

Hilaire Belloc

The holy passion of Friendship is of so sweet and steady
and loyal and enduring a nature that it will last through
a whole lifetime, if not asked to lend money.

Mark Twain

Each friend represents a world in us,
a world possibly not born until they
arrive, and it is only by this meeting
that a new world is born.

Anaïs Nin

HER FRIEND FLO

There is a dotty woman
Who when she does her shopping
And sees a hopscotch in the street
Goes hophop hophop hopping.

A game she often wins
Though no one else is there;
She plays a childhood friend, who'd now
Be quite as old as her.

And sometimes she denounces
That friend of long ago,
And says to all the empty air:
You *know* you cheated, Flo!

Gerda Mayer

We are always
the same age
inside.

Gertrude Stein

The joy of companionship with a feline friend is depicted in Athena's Mom by G. G. Kopilak.
Image from Private Collection/G. G. Kopilak/Superstock.

Remember When

SCHOOL
From *Lake Wobegon Days*
Garrison Keillor

School started the day after Labor Day, Tuesday, the Tuesday when my grandfather went, and in 1918 my father, and in 1948 me. It was the same day, in the same brick schoolhouse, the former New Albion Academy, now named Nelson School. The same misty painting of George Washington looked down on us all from above the blackboard, next to his closest friend, Abraham Lincoln. Lincoln was kind and patient and we looked to him for sympathy. Washington looked as if he had a headache. His mouth was set in a prim, pained expression of disapproval. Maybe people made fun of him for his long, frizzy hair, which resembled our teacher's, Mrs. Meiers's, and that had soured his disposition. She said he had bad

teeth—a good lesson for us to remember: to brush after every meal, up and down, thirty times. The great men held the room in their gaze, even the back corner by the windows. I bent over my desk, trying to make fat vowels sit on the line like fruit, the tails of consonants hang below, and colored the maps of English and French empires, and memorized arithmetic tables and state capitals and major exports of many lands, and when I was stumped, looked up to see George Washington's sour look and Lincoln's of pity and friendship, an old married couple on the wall. School, their old home, smelled of powerful floor wax and disinfectant, the smell of patriotism.

Mine was a vintage desk with iron scrollwork on the sides, an empty inkwell on top, a shelf below, lumps of

182   DOBBIN AND THE AUTOMOBILE

trip fo
to sta
early
time f
Now
the fai

petrified gum on the underside of it and some ancient inscriptions, one from '94 ("Lew P.") that made me think how old I'd be in '94 (fifty-two) and wonder who would have my place. I thought of leaving that child a message. A slip of paper stuck in a crack: "Hello. September 9, 1952. I'm in the fifth grade. It's sunny today. We had wieners for lunch and we played pom-pom-pullaway at recess. We are studying England. I hope you are well and enjoy school. If you find this, let me know. I'm 52 years old."...

It took me a long time to learn to read. I was wrong about so many words. Cat, can't. Tough, through, thought. Shinola. It was like reading a cloud of mosquitoes. Donna in the seat behind whispered right answers to me, and I learned to be a good guesser, but I didn't read well until Mrs. Meiers took me in hand.

One winter day she took me aside after recess and said she'd like me to stay after school and read to her. "You have such a nice voice," she said, "and I don't get to hear you read in school as much as I'd like."

No one had told me before that I had a nice voice. She told me many times over the next few months what a wonderful voice I had, as I sat in a chair by her desk reading to her as she marked worksheets. "The little duck was so happy. He ran to the barn and shouted, 'Come! Look! The ice is gone from the pond!' Finally it was spring."

"Oh, you read that so well. Read it again," she said. When Bill the janitor came in to mop, she said, "Listen to this. Doesn't this boy have a good voice?" He sat down and I read to them both. "The little duck climbed to the top of the big rock and looked down at the clear blue water. 'Now I am going to fly,' he said to himself. He waggled his wings and counted to three. 'One, two, three.' And he jumped and—" I read in my clear blue voice. "I think you're right," Bill said. "I think he has a very good voice. I wouldn't mind sitting here all day and listening to him."

AND THE AUTOMOBILE   183

bin. So, you see, you will have
y before Thanksgiving or very
ng morning if you are to be on
rkey.

put on the harness, and hitch
e to the buggy. He may jump

OUR HERITAGE

THE PLEDGE OF ALLEGIANCE

I pledge allegiance
to the flag
of the United States of America
and to the Republic
for which it stands,
one Nation under God,
indivisible, with liberty
and justice for all.

ABOUT THE TEXT

In 1892, in honor of the four hundredth anniversary of Christopher Columbus's arrival in the New World, President Benjamin Harrison proclaimed a national school celebration. For the occasion, Francis Bellamy, of Boston, Massachusetts, felt that the nation's school-children should state a simple yet heartfelt patriotic pledge, one that would be a part of a flag-raising ceremony. The now familiar Pledge of Allegiance was the result, and it first appeared in the September 1892 issue of The Youth's Companion, *of which Bellamy was editor. On Columbus Day of that year, children first recited America's Pledge of Allegiance in classrooms across the country.*

The Pledge has undergone some revisions in the past one hundred years. The original version was lengthened in 1923 and again in 1924. After the United States entered the second World War, Congress established guidelines for the treatment of the national flag, and included formal guidelines concerning reciting the Pledge of Allegiance. The proper position for reciting the pledge included standing with one's right hand over one's heart or, in the case of military personnel, at attention. Men were to remove their hats, and uniformed personnel were to salute. The year 1954 brought another revision to the Pledge when Congress voted to add two words: "under God." The Pledge was now not only a patriotic declaration, but a public prayer as well, one that all Americans continue to recite with pride.

A nineteenth-century schoolroom on a pioneer farm homestead in California stands ready for returning students. Photograph by W. Talarowski/H. Armstrong Roberts.

LEWIS AND CLARK

Dear Clark,

My friend . . . If there is anything in this enterprise, which would induce you to participate with me in its fatigues, its dangers and its honors, believe me there is no man on earth with whom I should feel equal pleasure in sharing them as with yourself.

Meriwether Lewis (From a letter written to William Clark, asking him to become part of an expedition into the Louisiana Territory)

Dear Lewis,

This is an undertaking fraught with many difficulties, but my friend, I do assure you that no man lives with whom I would prefer to undertake such a trip . . . as yourself.

William Clark (in reply to Lewis's letter)

A prominent American historian once called Meriwether Lewis's letter to William Clark asking him to become co-commander of an expedition into the Louisiana Territory "an invitation to greatness." Dramatic words, but misleading. Eventually, greatness would come to the two men but only after they led the "Corps of Discovery" across the continent in search of the fabled Northwest Passage to the Pacific Ocean. When Lewis wrote to Clark, he had no greatness to offer, only its uncertain promise and a long, dangerous journey. His letter was not a generous offer to a share of glory, but a shrewd request for help. Hand-picked and carefully prepared for the dangerous and unprecedented expedition by no less a man than President Thomas Jefferson. Lewis proved himself worthy of Jefferson's confidence before taking a single step into Louisiana when he acknowledged his need for help and asked his friend, William Clark, to be his partner.

Meriwether Lewis and William Clark had served together for six months in the United States Army, Clark as Lewis's commanding officer. Before the Corps of Discovery began their journey into the west in 1804, this was the extent of their time together—only six months. Apparently, this was enough time for the two to develop a mutual respect and affection, for both were eager to be partners in Jefferson's plan for exploration. On the surface, Lewis and Clark had much in common. Both were born in Virginia. Both were young—Lewis was twenty-nine when the trip began; Clark was thirty-three. And both were intelligent, resourceful, and courageous. They shared a spirit of adventure, and both had spent time on the frontier and were worthy woodsmen. But the men were near opposites in temperament. Lewis was a melancholy man, an introvert described by many as "troubled" or "dark." He was somewhat stiff and formal, highly educated and rather refined for an explorer. Clark, on the other had, was a steady tempered man, gregarious, pragmatic, and wise, a man given more to action than introspection.

The journals from the Corps of Discovery expedition prove that these two extraordinary men fell into perfect balance as they led their carefully selected group of thirty-two men straight into the unknown. Each day brought new discoveries, new dangers: the unexpected. They were tired, hungry, often ill, and always on guard against attack. They crossed treacherous mountains, survived freezing winters, and opened their eyes each morning to sights never before seen by American eyes. And in the journals of Lewis and Clark, and of the men under their command, there is mention of nary an argument, disagreement, or instance of second guessing between the two leaders. They were equals in command, equals in the eyes of the men, and, most importantly, equals in the eyes of each other. The most glaring instance of disagreement seems to have been over the question of meat eating—Lewis favored dog meat, while Clark found it unpalatable. Their united front was an inspiration to the men. At one point, when disagreement erupted as to which waterway was the true branch of the river they were following—some of the experienced rivermen insisted upon one direction, Lewis and Clark on the other—the men finally relented and agreed that, although they still held to their opinion, they would follow their united leaders any way they chose to go.

Lewis and Clark made each other better men.

Lewis taught Clark how to record celestial observation with a sextant; Clark taught Lewis how to navigate the western waterways. When Clark's feet were torn and bloodied by blisters after long hard days of walking, Lewis bathed and bandaged them. When Lewis suffered violent stomach distress, Clark offered a string of remedies—none truly effective, but each given with the greatest affection and care. The two men became like one man, a man who was stronger, smarter, and more capable than either alone.

Few other accomplishments in American history have been so significant to the nation's development than the journey of Lewis and Clark. The trip filled in our national map and opened wide our national imagination. But their heroism has lessons beyond the courage and glory of exploration. Lewis and Clark were friends, true friends. When Lewis asked Clark to become his co-commander, he invited him on board as an equal; and to make that equality official, he requested that his friend be given the same military rank as he had been granted. This is how the men of the Corps of Discovery knew their leaders—Captains Lewis and Clark. In truth, when Clark's commission came, it was as a lieutenant, technically a second-in-command to Lewis. Lewis apologized to his friend and insisted that the news be kept between them; in the eyes of the men and in the reality of the day-to-day expedition, the two would remain co-commanders. Lewis stuck to his word. There was no pulling of rank and no second guessing.

After the expedition was completed, Lewis repeatedly petitioned President Jefferson to remedy the official inequality between himself and Clark, and insisted over and again that his co-commander be given equal credit for their accomplishments. Greatness had been achieved, and Lewis was determined it would be shared. In fact, it was Meriwether Lewis who first used the term every American schoolchild has learned for almost two hundred years. He named their journey of exploration the "Lewis and Clark" expedition, guaranteeing that in the American mind, the two names would meld into one, and that history would always remember their journey as a partnership between friends.

_____

Nancy Skarmeas is a book editor and mother of a toddler, Gordon, who keeps her and her husband quite busy at their home in New Hampshire. Her Greek and Irish ancestry fostered a lifelong interest in research and history.

Grace's Friends

"Your walk is lonely, blue-eyed Grace,
Down the long forest-road to school
Where shadows troop, at a dismal pace,
From sullen chasm to sunless pool.
Are you not often, little maid,
Beneath the sighing trees afraid?"

"Afraid—beneath the tall, strong trees
That bend their arms to shelter me
And whisper down, with dew and breeze,
Sweet sounds that float on lovingly
Till every gorge and cavern seems
Thrilled through and through
        with fairy dreams?

"Afraid—beside the water dim
That holds the baby-lilies white
Upon its bosom, where a hymn
Ripples forth softly to the light
That now and then comes gliding in,
A lily's budding smile to win?

"Fast to the slippery precipice
I see the nodding harebell cling:
In that blue eye no fear there is;
Its hold is firm—the frail, free thing!
The harebell's Guardian cares for me:
So I am in safe company.

"The woodbine clambers up the cliff
And seems to murmur, 'Little Grace,
The sunshine were less welcome if
It brought not every day your face.'
Red leaves slip down from maples high
And touch my cheek as they flit by.

"I feel at home with everything
That has its dwelling in the wood;
With flowers that laugh and birds that sing—

Companions beautiful and good,
Brothers and sisters everywhere;
And over all, our Father's care.

"In rose-time or in berry-time—
When ripe seeds fall or buds peep out—
While green the turf or white the rime,
There's something to be glad about.
It makes my heart bound, just to pass
The sunbeams dancing on the grass.

"And when the bare rocks shut me in
Where not a blade of grass will grow,
My happy fancies soon begin
To warble music, rich and low,
And paint what eyes could never see:
My thoughts are company for me.

"What does it mean to be alone?
And how is any one afraid
Who feels the dear God on His throne
Sending His sunshine through the shade,
Warming the damp sod into bloom,
And smiling off the thicket's gloom?

"At morning, down the wood-path cool
The fluttering leaves make cheerful talk;
After the stifled day at school,
I hear, along my homeward walk,
The airy wisdom of the wood—
Far easiest to be understood.

"I whisper to the winds; I kiss
The rough old oak and clasp his bark;
No farewell of the thrush I miss;
I lift the soft veil of the dark
And say to bird and breeze and tree,
'Good night! Good friends you are to me!'"

Autumn leaves in brilliant color adorn a quiet lane in Bristol, Maine. Photograph by Dick Dietrich.

Lucy Larcom

Friendship is
Love
Without His Wings

Why should my anxious breast repine,
Because my youth is fled?
Days of delight may still be mine;
Affection is not dead.
In tracing back the years of youth,
One firm record, one lasting truth
Celestial consolation brings;
Bear it, ye breezes, to the seat
Where first my heart responsive beat.—
"Friendship is Love without his wings!"

Through few, but checkered years,
What moments have been mine!
Now half obscured by clouds of tears,
Now bright in rays divine;
Howe'er my future doom be cast,
My soul, enraptured with the past,
To one idea fondly clings;
Friendship! that thought is all thine own,
Worth worlds of bliss, that thought alone—
"Friendship is Love without his wings!"

George Gordon, Lord Byron

A harvest wreath welcomes visitors to a country home. Photograph by Nancy Matthews.

THE MONK AND THE PEASANT

A peasant once unthinkingly
    Spread tales about a friend;
But later found the rumors false
    And hoped to make amend.

He sought the counsel of a monk,
    A man esteemed and wise,
Who heard the peasant's story through
    And felt he must advise.

The kind monk said: "If you would have
    A mind again at peace,
I have a plan whereby you may
    From trouble find release.

"Go fill a bag with chicken-down
    And to each door-yard go
And lay one fluffy feather where
    The streams of gossip flow."

The peasant did as he was told
    And to the monk returned,
Elated that his penance was
    A thing so quickly earned.

"Not yet," the old monk sternly said,
    "Take up your bag once more
And gather up the feathers that
    Were placed at every door."

The peasant, eager to atone,
    Went hastening to obey;
No feathers met his sight, the wind
    Had blown them all away.

Margaret E. Bruner

Autumn-colored ivy clings to a well-weathered door in Multnomah County, Oregon. Photograph by Steve Terrill.

A
SLICE OF LIFE

— Edgar A. Guest —

FRIENDS

Ain't it fine when things are going
    Topsy-turvy and askew
To discover someone showing
    Good old-fashioned faith in you?

Ain't it good when life seems dreary
    And your hopes about to end,
Just to feel the handclasp cheery
    Of a fine old loyal friend?

Gosh! one fellow to another
    Means a lot from day to day,
Seems we're living for each other
    In a friendly sort of way.

When a smile or cheerful greetin'
    Means so much to fellow sore,
Seems we ought to keep repeatin'
    Smiles an' praises more an' more.

Edgar A. Guest began his illustrious career in 1895 at the age of fourteen when his work first appeared in the Detroit Free Press. *His column was syndicated in over three hundred newspapers, and he became known as "The Poet of the People."*

Devotions FROM THE Heart

Pamela Kennedy

"I . . . cease not to give thanks for you,
making mention of you in my prayers."
Ephesians 1:15, 16

PRAYING FRIENDS

I met an old friend for lunch the other day and we spent a couple of hours catching up on things. Our children are now young adults and are launching out on lives of their own at college or in the workplace. An engagement has just been announced and decisions about jobs are under consideration. As mothers are prone to do, we discussed our thoughts and opinions about their lives. As realists, however, we knew our input at this point in our children's lives might certainly be taken as meddling. So we spoke with one another instead, bouncing ideas back and forth. When we parted that afternoon my friend took my hand briefly and smiled.

"I'll be praying," she whispered.

I squeezed her hand in return and responded, "Me too."

It was a simple and short exchange, but it held the essence of our friendship. In all the years we have been friends, we have supported one another in prayer. When we were each newlyweds and our husbands were sent overseas to war, the reassurance of our mutual prayers helped us through the darkest times. When infertility filled my days with tears, the prayers of my friend gave me the strength to carry on. We rejoiced in praise and thanksgiving when her husband successfully recovered from a stroke and beseeched God for his wisdom when a rebellious child threatened to tear the family apart. We knew we didn't have the answers for one another but took comfort in the assurance that we knew the One who did. And in the years we have upheld each other, our friendship has grown deeper, strengthened by the cords of prayer. In the act of

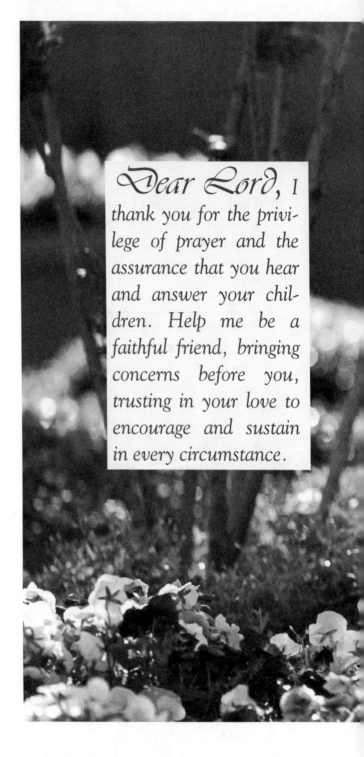

Dear Lord, I thank you for the privilege of prayer and the assurance that you hear and answer your children. Help me be a faithful friend, bringing concerns before you, trusting in your love to encourage and sustain in every circumstance.

bringing one another before the throne of God, we have learned what it is to be a better friend.

It is comforting to hear someone say they wish you well or will be thinking about you. A cheerful note or phone call "just to see how things are going" is always welcome, but the empathy and compassion in the commitment to pray elevates friendship to a level above the ordinary. It lifts the heart and soul with the knowledge that your cares will be brought before the God of heaven who knows and loves you more than any person ever

Two friends share good conversation as they work in the garden. Photograph by Uniphoto.

could. It indicates a dedication born of loving concern. And in a world where time is of the essence, the promise of prayer reminds us of a place where eternity reigns supreme.

Sometimes, when faced with another's pain or need, we are overwhelmed. We may feel powerless to help or at a loss to offer advice. Some situations require experience or wisdom we do not possess. The beauty of prayer is that it is not limited by our limitations. Prayer brings access to the abundance of God. It does not require a degree in theology or experience in counseling but only the willingness to listen and share our concerns with the Lord. Prayer requires no special equipment and is not defined by our location. On the wings of prayer we are transported beyond ourselves.

As friends we enjoy opportunities to share laughter and tears, memories and dreams, to hold a hand or offer a hug. But there is something more we can do for one another out of love; we can exercise the precious privilege of lifting one another in the arms of prayer.

MESSAGE

For one to bear my message, I looked out
In haste, at noon. The bee and swallow passed
Bound south. My message was to South. I cast
It, trusting as a mariner, no doubt,
Sweet bee blithe swallow, in my heart about
Your fellowship.

    The stealthy night came fast.
"O chilly night," I said, "no friend thou hast
For me, and morn is far," when lo! a shout
Of joy, and riding up as one rides late,
My friend fell on my neck just in the gate.
"You got my message then?"

    "No message, sweet,
Save my own eyes' desire your eyes to meet."
"You saw no swallow and no bee before
You came?"
    "I do remember past my door
There brushed a bird and bee. O dearer presage
Than I had dreamed! You sent them by a message?"

Helen Jackson

Artist Pierre Auguste Renoir captures the close-knit bond of best friends in this painting,
Title Unknown (Two Girls Talking). Image from Private Collection/Superstock.

Letter Openers

by Erica Cartman

Right after we were married, my husband and I spent a year apart as I finished graduate school in Virginia while he began a new job in Boston. I was lonely that year, anxious to get on with my new life, and feeling more than a little bit cheated to have had my married life interrupted before it had even begun. But the separation had its positive side, for I discovered something about my husband that year that I had never known—he was a wonderful letter writer. Alone and occasionally feeling quite sorry for myself, I grabbed onto his letters like a lifeline. I made a whole ritual out of collecting the mail. I would walk to the post office at the same time every afternoon—holding off until the end of the day to savor the anticipation—and then I would tuck the pile of mail inside my big leather book bag and carry it to a little coffee shop on campus. Only then would I sort through the pile and look for that familiar handwriting on steel gray stationary. For added drama, sometime during the year I began opening his letters with an old wooden letter opener I had found at a flea market in town. It was carved from some unidentifiable type of wood and had once had an intricately carved design on the handle end, although most of that was lost to wear by the time I laid eyes on it. With a flourish of graduate student affectation, I would open each of my husband's letters with that opener; and I would use it on no other piece of mail. It all seems a bit silly looking back, but I was lonely, and those letters were truly an oasis of comfort.

Those days of separation seem so long ago now. Twenty years later and under the same roof for a long, long time, my husband and I live lives so full of togetherness that I find myself remembering those quiet afternoons in the coffee shop with a strange sense of longing. Today there are jobs and children and schools and neighbors and meetings and endless lists of responsibilities. But old habits die hard. I no longer count on letters to get me through the day, but I do still cherish them. When an envelope arrives bearing familiar handwriting—from my sister on the west coast, or from one of my many far-flung friends—I anxiously await a break in the action so I can retreat to my study and savor the moment. And I still use letter openers. I never was able to part with that old wooden letter opener from my graduate school days, and, through the years, I have become somewhat of a collector of these often neglected items. I buy them everywhere—antique shops (where they are always among the lowest priced items), flea markets, yard sales. They are not a collectible that makes great demands upon the collector. Most cost only a few dollars—except for those of precious metals decorated with gems, which are not among my collection—and they are not difficult to find, although they are often relegated to some dark corners of the shop or a big box of odds and ends at a yard sale. I keep my collection in an old wooden box on my desk. Not on display, just on reserve until a worthy letter arrives. I have a set of Fuller Brush openers in colorful plastic, made during the post World War II years when plastic letter openers became a favorite means of cheap advertising. I have openers made of wood, bone, bark, and all type and colors of plastic. Many were advertisements, some were book marks, a few even doubled as ball point pens until their ink dried up. None are of any great monetary value. But I love them nonetheless, because I love letters.

It's funny, my husband, whose beautifully written letters are really responsible for my devotion to letter openers, can't understand my fascination either with letters or with the collection of devices I keep to open them. (Maybe I was so caught up in the pleasure of reading his letters all those years ago that I did an entirely uninspired job of writing my replies!) To him, mail means only bills and bad news, better left unopened. Letter openers, he says, only prolong an unpleasant process. And I suppose he is right, except that I would never use any of my letter openers on a mere bill or a piece of junk mail. I keep them true to their intended purpose—they open letters, with just enough flourish to mark the moment as special.

A SLICE OF HISTORY

If you would like to begin collecting antique letter openers, here are some interesting facts:

HISTORY
•In the twelfth century, when Europeans began making paper, letters were written on large pieces of paper and folded into a square or rectangle with the writing inside. A drop of melted wax sealed the folds and one's personal seal, usually cast in a ring, was pressed into the wax. A "paper knife" was used to break the seal of the letter. This tool was later renamed a "letter opener" because its original use was to open letters, not envelopes.
•Handmade envelopes, still using a wax seal, were used in the sixteenth century but were not in high demand because most of the population remained illiterate.
•Letter openers gained in popularity as literacy increased throughout the eighteenth century.
•By 1860, letter openers were owned and used by virtually everyone, mainly because of an invention in 1840 of an envelope machine and by Congress who, in 1851, authorized the printing of pre-stamped envelopes.
•After the Civil War, as people began moving west and the railroad system grew, letters became the main source of communication for every class. Traveling desks, along with smaller, lighter letter openers, were carried by many American travelers.
•On October 1, 1867, G. C. Barney received the first patent on a letter opener. His design resembled a can opener with its hooked end.
•In the 1880s, advertising letter openers were a popular premium offered by all kinds of businesses, (most of which had no connection to writing or letters).
•With the invention and accessibility of the telephone, letter openers lost the popularity they once possessed as an advertising tool. Double-purpose openers (with a ballpoint pen,

A collection of antique letter openers adorns a writer's desk. Photograph by Jessie Walker.

bookmark, magnifying glass, etc. on one end) were produced in an attempt to boost sales.

MATERIALS AND DESIGN
•"Paper knives" or "letter knives" can be found in silver, gold, ivory, tortoise, bone, shell, jade, and mother of pearl. They may contain semi-precious jewels, family crests, one's initials, or figurines on the end, with owls, dogs, foxes, and cats being the most desirable by collectors.
•Lithographed tin was used for advertising letter openers in the 1890s, whereas after World War II, impressed plastic became popular.
•Styles of letter openers and the materials used to make them reflected their time period. Celluloid was often used for Art Nouveau style openers in the early 1900s; Bakelite was used for Art Deco style openers in the 1920s and 1930s, and simple plastic and metal openers were popular in the 1950s.

Andrea Zywicki

Desk

My desk, most loyal friend,
      thank you. You've been with me on
every road I've taken.
      My scar and my protection.

My loaded writing mule.
      Your tough legs have endured
the weight of all my dreams, and
      burdens of piled-up thoughts.

Thank you for toughening me.
      No worldly joy could pass
your severe looking-glass
      you blocked the first temptation,

and every base desire
      your heavy oak outweighed
lions of hate, elephants
      of spite you intercepted.

Thank you for growing with me
      as my need grew in size
I've been laid out across you
      so many years alive . . .

I celebrate thirty years
      of union truer than love
I know every notch in your wood.
      You know the lines in my face.

Haven't you written them there?
      devouring reams of paper
denying me any tomorrow
      teaching me only today.

You've thrown my important letters
      and money in floods together,
repeating: for every single verse
      today has to be the deadline.

You've warned me of retribution
      not to be measured in spoonfulls.
And when my body will be laid out,
      Great fool! Let it be on you then.

Marina Tsvetayeva

*An antique writing desk complete with quill pen and stationery awaits
the writer's return. Photograph by Jessie Walker.*

Mrs. Elizabeth Morgan
Wild Rose, Wisconsin

Dear Elizabeth

The summer flowers are beginning
to fade and soon the leaves will
turn to brilliant shades of red
and orange.

A tinwork letter box holds precious memories of years gone by. Photograph by Jerry Koser.

TINWORK LETTER BOX
Patricia Stone

When I learned last fall that one of my dearest childhood friends would be married this June, I knew I must make something truly special to mark the occasion. Clare and I had been neighbors from the age of eight— two of the only girls in a neighborhood with enough boys our age to field two full baseball teams on a summer afternoon. We were, in fact, very different. She played with dolls and wore dresses to school; I wore my brother's hand-me-downs and was determined to outplay every boy on the field. But still, we became friends. We lived only about two hundred yards from each other, at opposite ends of a circular drive. We couldn't look out the window and see each other's houses, but we could run the distance in a minute or two. So it might seem odd that we began a voluminous correspondence during the summer of our ninth year, but we did. We each had a brother who delivered the newspaper; they worked for competing papers and were up at dawn to run their routes. We enlisted them as our couriers. Each night, usually after a full day spent together, we would sit down in our rooms and write long notes to one another. What did we write? I can't remember a single word. All that I remember is how much we treasured that correspondence and how pleased we were to have this tangible evidence of the special bond between us. I kept Clare's notes from that summer, and from the many seasons that followed, in an old cigar box under my bed, safe from the family members I was sure were eager to read them and who, in truth, probably never gave them a second thought.

I was reminded of that secret correspondence not long after I received the news of Clare's engagement. Searching my craft books for just the right project, I came upon instructions for an embossed tin jewelry box. The decorative tin covered an old cigar box, just like the one that had held Clare's letters so many years ago. I had found the perfect gift for my dear old friend; but I wouldn't call it a jewelry box, my embossed tin box would be a letter box.

Tinwork, I discovered, is thousands of years old. The ancient Romans discovered vast tin deposits in the area around Cornwall, England, in the second century B.C. and began a thriving tin trade that continued well into the eighteenth century A.D. Tin was exported from England all around the world. Craftspeople turned it into practical domestic items, mixed it with other metals to produce durable and beautiful alloys, and used it as the raw material for works of fine art. In early America, tin was very popular for domestic items like candlesticks, lanterns, and utensils. Colonial craftspeople used piercing and punching techniques to decorate their tinwork, creating works of folk art that are much sought after by collectors today. In the nineteenth cen-

tury, practical innovations allowed for tin items to be machine produced, and handcrafters began to disappear. Eventually, aluminum replaced tin for most practical purposes, leaving the ancient metal to be rediscovered by late twentieth century craftspeople, who have begun to turn their creative minds toward this simple ancient medium.

A local cigar store was happy to give me as many old cigar boxes as I wanted, although some stores do charge a nominal fee. Procuring tin foil of the correct thickness proved more challenging, but I found .005-inch aluminum foil at a hardware store (a metal supplier in your area may carry the foil if you cannot find it at the hardware store). The design I used to emboss the top of the letter box I borrowed from an old book of quilting patterns that my grandmother had given me. I traced the quilt pattern onto a piece of tracing paper and then transferred the design onto the foil. The embossing process is really very simple: using a pencil or an empty ballpoint pen, trace the design onto the dull side of the foil. Turn the foil over and paint highlights with an enamel paint (I used gold). Let the paint dry completely and then glue the foil onto your cigar box, which I had covered with black fabric beforehand.

Once I'd finished the box I realized that it wasn't really appropriate as a formal wedding gift for Clare and her husband; it was instead a personal offering from me to her. Our friendship has had so many opportunities to falter—separate high schools, far away colleges, changing jobs, changing addresses, my marriage and children, and now her marriage. Each new twist in our lives has pulled us farther apart physically; but never has the emotional bond between us been broken. So I hope that my dear old friend will treasure this letter box in the spirit that I created it, as a tribute to our childhood correspondence and to our lifelong friendship, to a bond formed in the long ago days when the world was new to us, exciting and scary all at once, and a good friend was the most important thing of all.

FRIENDSHIP'S ROAD

I've a warm and friendly feeling
    As I think of you today;
And I wish that we could visit,
    But you're many miles away.

Separated by such distance,
    Yet your letters bring you near;
Through the miles we share a friendship
    That's become to me most dear.

Friends through correspondence only;
    Still, your face I need not see
For your soul shines through the pages
    Every time you write to me.

You've a special way of writing,
    Warming as the sunshine rays
Bringing joy and inspiration,
    Letters brightening up my days.

You've enriched my life, my dear one,
    And I'm glad God willed we meet.
"Friendship's road" is that much nicer
    Traveling it with one so sweet.

Beverly J. Anderson

Mementos from years of correspondence provide a pansy-lover with a treasure trove of memories. Photograph by Nancy Matthews.

To an Heirloom Teapot

They tell me that a hundred years ago
A great-great-grandma handled you with grace
As cordially she nodded to each guest
While cups were passed around from place to place.
Upon your face quaint maids and urchins play
On grassy terraces in dull old blue;
They beckon me to come and join their pranks
As they have done to all who handled you.
We somehow sense the chatter and the charm
Of those who circled round your generous self.
What you could tell!—No wonder we are proud
To give you honored place upon our shelf.

Marie Hunter Dawson

Nothing is ever lost by courtesy. It is the cheapest of the pleasures; costs nothing and conveys much. It pleases him who gives and him who receives, and thus, like mercy, it is twice blessed.

Erastus Wiman

*A china tea set awaits the arrival of guests for an afternoon tea party.
Photograph by Nancy Matthews.*

Family Recipes

Snickerdoodles

½ cup butter
1½ cups all-purpose flour
1 cup sugar
1 egg
½ teaspoon vanilla

¼ teaspoon baking soda
¼ teaspoon cream of tartar
2 tablespoons sugar
1 teaspoon ground cinnamon

In a large mixing bowl, cream butter until light. Add half of the flour and mix well. Add 1 cup sugar, egg, vanilla, baking soda, and cream of tartar. Beat until thoroughly combined, scraping sides of bowl occasionally. Stir in remaining flour. Cover and chill for 1 hour.

Preheat oven to 375° F. In a shallow dish, combine 2 tablespoons sugar and cinnamon.

Shape dough into 1-inch balls. Roll in sugar mixture to coat. Place 2 inches apart on ungreased cookie sheet and bake 10 minutes. Cool on cookie sheet for 1 minute then remove to a wire rack. Makes about 3 dozen.

Kim Bennett
Raleigh, North Carolina

Lemon-Coconut Bars

⅓ cup butter
1 cup sugar, divided
1 cup plus 2 tablespoons
all-purpose flour, divided
2 eggs

2 teaspoons lemon zest
3 tablespoons fresh lemon juice
½ teaspoon baking powder
1 cup shredded coconut
Powdered sugar

Preheat oven to 350° F. In a medium bowl, cream butter with ¼ cup of the sugar until light and fluffy. Add 1 cup of the flour and mix until mixture resembles fine crumbs. Press mixture into an ungreased 8-inch square baking pan. Bake 15 minutes.

In a medium mixing bowl, beat eggs until foamy. Add remaining sugar, 2 tablespoons flour, lemon juice, baking powder,

and salt. Beat about 3 minutes or until slightly thickened. Stir in lemon peel and coconut. Pour mixture over crust. Bake 20 to 25 minutes or until slightly golden around the edges and center is set. Cool on wire rack. Sift powdered sugar over top and cut into bars. Store covered, in refrigerator. Makes 16 servings.

Liesl Prater
Atlanta, Georgia

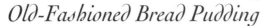

Old-Fashioned Bread Pudding

6 stale biscuits, torn into small pieces
2 eggs
¾ cup sugar

2 cups milk
½ cup raisins, if desired
1 teaspoon vanilla extract

In a large bowl, tear biscuits into bite-sized pieces; set aside. In a medium bowl, lightly beat eggs; add sugar and mix well. Stir in milk, raisins, and vanilla. Pour over biscuits and stir to mix. Pour into a buttered casserole dish; set aside. Preheat oven to 350° F. Bake 45 minutes until a toothpick inserted in the middle comes out clean. Serve warm or cold. Recipe can be doubled. Makes 6-8 servings.

Martha Henry Hall
Malvern, Arkansas

Caramel Apple Oat Squares

1¾ cups all-purpose flour
1 cup quick-cooking oats
½ cup packed brown sugar
½ teaspoon baking soda
½ teaspoon salt

1 cup cold margarine
1 cup chopped walnuts
20 caramels, unwrapped
1 14-ounce can sweetened condensed milk
1 21-ounce can apple pie filling

Preheat oven to 375° F. In a large bowl, combine flour, oats, sugar, baking soda, and salt. Cut in margarine until crumbly. Reserve 1½ cups crumb mixture. Press the remainder of the mixture on the bottom of a 9-by-13-inch baking pan. Bake 15 minutes. Remove from oven.

To reserved crumb mixture, add walnuts and set aside. In a heavy saucepan, combine caramels and sweetened condensed milk. Place pan over low heat. Stirring mixture constantly, heat until smooth. Remove from heat. Spoon apple pie filling over the baked crust, top with caramel mixture, then reserved crumb and nut mixture. Bake 20 minutes or until set. Serve warm with ice cream. Makes about 2 dozen.

Lois Donoho
Varna, Illinois

Spicy Gingerbread

1 cup packed brown sugar
1 cup molasses
½ cup melted butter
2 eggs
¾ cup milk
1 tablespoon lemon juice

3 cups all-purpose flour
1 teaspoon baking soda
2 teaspoons ground ginger
1½ teaspoon ground cinnamon
1 teaspoon ground cloves
Whipped cream, if desired

Preheat oven to 350° F. In a large bowl, mix sugar, molasses, and butter; beat well. Add eggs, one at a time, beating well after each. Set aside. In a small bowl, mix lemon juice and milk. Set aside. In a medium bowl, sift together flour, baking soda, ginger, cinnamon, and cloves. Add dry ingredients to egg mixture alternating with milk mixture. Mix thoroughly. Pour batter into a greased 9-by-13-inch baking pan. Bake 25 to 30 minutes. Cool. Top with whipped cream, if desired. Makes about 2 dozen.

Chris Bryant
Johnson City, Tennessee

THROUGH MY WINDOW

Pamela Kennedy

Art by Patrick McRae

MY BODY, MY FRIEND

In the summer of my fiftieth year, I set out with my second son to tour colleges. He was ready to begin his senior year in high school and wanted to make some decisions about higher education. We selected five universities in our home state of Washington and headed off for a week of visitation. After driving hundreds of miles around the Evergreen State and walking for hours over rolling grassy hills, across brick quadrangles and up thousands of stairs, our young scholar made his decision. I also made a decision. My body was betraying me! Despite my youthful outlook on life,

physically I was falling apart! It was clear I needed to change some things if I wanted to enjoy the last half of my life as much as the first!

Arriving home after our trek, I called up the local gym and fitness center and made an appointment with a counselor. When we met I shared my concerns and suggested perhaps I could benefit from getting into better shape. She listened attentively, took some notes, and then asked a few questions:

"What kind of exercise program have you done in the past?" she asked.

"Well, I vacuum and dust. Oh, and I make a

big shopping trip to the grocery store once a week. Lots of loading and unloading the car involved."

"And how do you prepare your meals?" she inquired.

"Well, I fix good, balanced meals. Meat, potatoes, homemade desserts, and so forth."

"Hmm." She made a few notes and gave me a quick once over with her well-trained eyes. "I think you could really benefit from a course in nutrition along with a regular workout routine involving weight lifting and aerobic exercise."

"Oh, I was thinking along the lines of a diet pill and some recreational walking." I offered.

"I believe in a more natural route to health," she countered.

I was certain this involved hard work, sweat, and commitment—three things I didn't particularly enjoy. I looked into her sparkling, dark eyes and sighed. Well, my route to physical fitness hadn't worked for the first fifty years of my life, perhaps I'd give hers a try.

Within a week my perky little trainer had me counting the fat grams and carbohydrates on every box, bag, and can I picked up at the grocery store. She quickly dispatched my contention that tasting food while preparing it was not really eating and destroyed my happy notion that "low-fat" on the label means I can eat as much as I want. I learned to substitute applesauce for oil in baking and whole grains for processed flour, fake eggs for real and chicken broth for butter when mashing potatoes. I learned why angel food cake paves the way to dieter's heaven, while devil's food will send you straight to the pit! It became an adventure to take an old recipe and "slenderize" it. Most of the time it worked, but I drew the line at turkey burgers laced with sprouts.

Exercise and I have never been the best of friends, so I was hopeful that redesigning my diet would accomplish my goals. My trainer, Sara, threw that idea out the window by informing me that working out was the only sure route to the promised land of physical fitness. She introduced me to the equipment and I soon learned that barbells don't ring and a moving treadmill belt waits for no woman. When it starts, you go or find your-self dumped off in a heap! I tried the high-tech video bikes, but I could never keep them on the video road and constantly ran into video trees, buildings, and vehicles, filling the room with video crashing sounds. I didn't need the humiliation. I gave the air-stepper a try but got a terrible cramp in my arms from supporting my leaden legs as they refused to climb past the tenth floor. Finally, I returned to the treadmill, where I could stare at a strategically placed television screen and watch the news while my lower body took on a life of its own. It kept my mind off my reluctant muscles.

I expected to see speedy results from my new, healthier lifestyle, but in the first few weeks my progress was slow. The only real benefit I could identify was the feeling of euphoria I experienced each day when my hour of torture at the gym was over. Then, little by little, I began to notice changes. I seemed to have more energy. I didn't have to pull so hard at the waistbands of my skirts and jeans in order to get them fastened. I could run up the stairs at home without having to pause at the top to catch my breath. I could even hold a note longer at choir practice! Friends noticed a change in me too and I can't describe the feeling I got from buying a dress in a new and smaller size! I even decided to try out a new hairstyle.

One day, while getting dressed, I glanced at myself in the mirror and realized that I didn't mind what I saw there! My curves were a little straighter and muscles were appearing here and there. The body I had held in disdain just a few months ago didn't look too bad. Now with every bit of success, I am encouraged to continue—to lift ten more pounds, to turn down that piece of cheesecake in favor of fresh fruit, to run up the stairs instead of hopping in the elevator. After all, my body and I will probably be together for many more years. We might as well learn to be friends!

Pamela Kennedy is a freelance writer of short stories, articles, essays, and children's books. Wife of a retired naval officer and mother of three children, she has made her home on both U.S. coasts and currently resides in Kent, Washington.

LITTLE AND GREAT

A traveler on a dusty road
　Strewed acorns on the lea;
And one took root and sprouted up,
　And grew into a tree.
Love sought its shade at evening-time,
　To breathe its early vows;
And Age was pleased, in heats of noon,
　To bask beneath its boughs.
The dormouse loved its dangling twigs,
　The birds sweet music bore—
It stood a glory in its place,
　A blessing evermore.

A little spring had lost its way
　Amid the grass and fern;
A passing stranger scooped a well
　Where weary men might turn;
He walled it in, and hung with care
　A ladle at the brink;
He thought not of the deed he did,
　But judged that Toil might drink.
He passed again; and lo! the well,
　By summer never dried,
Had cooled ten thousand parchèd tongues,
　And saved a life beside.

A dreamer dropped a random thought;
　'Twas old, and yet 'twas new;
A simple fancy of the brain,
　But strong in being true.
It shone upon a genial mind,
　And, lo! its light became
A lamp of life, a beacon ray,
　A monitory flame:
The thought was small; its issue great;
　A watch-fire on the hill,
It sheds its radiance far adown,
　And cheers the valley still.

A nameless man, amid the crowd
　That thronged the daily mart,
Let fall a word of hope and love,
　Unstudied from the heart;—
A whisper on the tumult thrown,
　A transitory breath,—
It raised a brother from the dust,
　It saved a soul from death.
O germ! O fount! O word of love!
　O thought at random cast!
Ye were but little at the first,
　But mighty at the last.

Charles Mackay

A stroller takes a late morning walk down Hart Prairie Road in Flagstaff, Arizona. Photograph by Dick Dietrich.

TRAVELER'S Diary

from DOMESTIC MANNERS OF THE AMERICANS
Frances Trollope

Our Autumn walks were delightful; the sun ceased to scorch; the want of flowers was no longer peculiar to Ohio; and the trees took a colouring, which in richness, brilliance, and variety, exceeded all description. I think it is the maple, or sugar-tree, that first sprinkles the forest with rich crimson; the beech follows, with all its harmony of golden tints, from pale yellow up to brightest orange. The dog-wood gives almost the purple colour of the mulberry; the chestnut softens all with its frequent mass of delicate brown, and the sturdy oak carries its deep green into the very lap of winter. These tints are too bright for the landscape painter; the attempt to follow nature in an American autumn scene must be abortive. The colours are in reality extremely brilliant, but the medium through which they are seen increases the effect surprisingly. Of all the points in which America has the advantage of England, the one I felt most sensibly was the clearness and brightness of the atmosphere. By day and by night this exquisite purity of air gives tenfold beauty to every object. I could hardly believe the stars were the same; the Great Bear looked like a constellation of suns; and Jupiter justified all the fine things said of him in those beautiful lines, from I know not what spirited pen, beginning,

I looked on thee, Jove! till my gaze
Shrunk, smote by the pow'r of thy blaze.

I always remarked that the first silver line of the moon's crescent attracted the eye on the first day, in America, as strongly as it does here on the third. I observed another phenomenon in the crescent moon of that region, the cause of which I less understood. That appearance which Shakespeare describes as "the new moon, with the old moon in her lap," and which I have heard ingeniously explained as the effect of *earth light,* was less visible there than here.

Cuyp's clearest landscapes have an atmosphere that approaches nearer to that of America than any I remember on canvas; but even Cuyp's *air* cannot reach the lungs, and, therefore, can only give an idea of half the enjoyment; for it makes itself felt as well as seen, and is indeed a constant source of pleasure.

Frances Trollope (1780–1863) was a prolific novelist, but it was her travel book, Domestic Manners of the Americans, *excerpted here, that won her critical acclaim. Trollope traveled to the United States from her native England at age forty-eight to save her family from financial ruin. While her many business ventures failed, her writing kept the family going.*

A vibrant red maple shelters a delicate fern. Photograph by William Johnson/Johnson's Photography.

Leaves
Compared with Flowers

A tree's leaves may be ever so good,
So may its bark, so may its wood;
But unless you put the right thing to its root
It never will show much flower or fruit.

But I may be one who does not care
Ever to have tree bloom or bear.
Leaves for smooth and bark for rough,
Leaves and bark may be tree enough.

Some giant trees have bloom so small
They might as well have none at all.
Late in life I have come on fern.
Now lichens are due to have their turn.

I bade men tell me which in brief,
Which is fairer, flower or leaf,
They did not have the wit to say,
Leaves by night and flowers by day.

Leaves and bark, leaves and bark,
To lean against and hear in the dark.
Petals I may have once pursued.
Leaves are all my darker mood.

Robert Frost

Vine maple trees transform into a kaleidoscope of color in the Willamette Valley, Oregon. Background photograph by Steve Terrill. Close-up photograph by Bruce Jackson/Jon Gnass Photo Images.

VESTIGIA

I took a day to search for God
And found Him not. But as I trod
    By rocky ledge, through woods untamed,
    Just where one scarlet lily flamed,
I saw His footprint in the sod.

Then suddenly, all unaware,
Far off in the deep shadows where
    A solitary hermit thrush
    Sang through the holy twilight hush—
I heard His voice upon the air.

And even as I marveled how
God gives us heaven, here and now,
    In a stir of wind that hardly shook
    The poplar leaves beside the brook—
His hand was light upon my brow.

At last with evening I turned
Homeward, and thought what I had learned
    And all that there was still to probe—
    I caught the glory of His robe
Where the last fires of sunset burned.

Back to the world with quickening start
I looked and longed for any part
    In making saving beauty be—
    And from that kindly ecstasy
I knew God dwelt within my heart.

Bliss Carman

*A hiker pauses to enjoy the beauty of Whitaker Point in the
Upper Buffalo Wilderness of the Ozark National Forest, Arkansas.
Photograph by H. Abernathy/H. Armstrong Roberts.*

Readers' Forum

Snapshots from Our Ideals Readers

ABOVE: Melanie MacMullan strolls down the garden path with her grandmother's golden retriever, Molly. Melanie and Molly are both two years old and the best of friends. Melanie lives with her parents, Sam and Donna MacMullan, and big sister Sarah in Colombia, Maryland. Proud grandparents are Lou and Sue Gonsalves from Hellertown, Pennsylvania. Melanie is the youngest of four grandchildren.

RIGHT: Cheryl Bazzoui of Bradford, Pennsylvania, sent in this snapshot of her one-year-old grandson Ethan. Grandmother Cheryl says that Ethan is a sweet, inquisitive little guy.

THANK YOU Lou and Sue Gonsalves, Cheryl Bazzoui, Ida Deck, and Jan Bass for sharing your family photographs with *Ideals*. We hope to hear from other readers who would like to share snapshots with the *Ideals* family. Please include a self-addressed, stamped envelope if you would like the photos returned. Keep your original photographs for safekeeping and send duplicate photos along with your name, address, and telephone number to:

READERS' FORUM
IDEALS PUBLICATIONS INC.
P.O. BOX 305300
NASHVILLE, TENNESSEE 37230

ideals®

Publisher, Patricia A. Pingry

Editor, Lisa C. Ragan

Prepress Manager, Eve DeGrie

Editorial Assistant, Andrea Zywicki

Contributing Editors, Lansing Christman, Deana Deck, Pamela Kennedy, Patrick McRae, Nancy Skarmeas

ABOVE: *Ideals* reader Ida Deck painted this tiny tea set as a gift to grandparents Alice and Jerry Deck of Okemos, Michigan, to celebrate the birth of their granddaughter Hannah Davis. When Hannah was two years old, she had a tea party with Grandmother Alice. Hannah is the daughter of Sarah and Jason Davis of Williamston, Michigan.

LEFT: Jan Bass of Council Bluffs, Iowa, sent us this picture of her grand*pup*, Nikita. Jan says Nikita is a very smart dog and even knows to take time to smell the flowers!

ACKNOWLEDGMENTS

END OF SUMMER by Rowena Bastin Bennett. From *JACK AND JILL*, copyright © 1949 by Curtis Publishing Company. Used by permission of Children's Better Health Institute, Benjamin Franklin Literary & Medical Society, Inc., Indianapolis, Indiana. TREE AT MY WINDOW and LEAVES COMPARED WITH FLOWERS from *COLLECTED POEMS OF ROBERT FROST*, edited by Edward Connery Lathem, Copyright © 1936, 1956 by Robert Frost. Copyright © 1964 by Lesley Frost Ballantine. Copyright © 1928, 1969 by Henry Holt & Company. Reprinted by permission of Henry Holt and Company, Inc. Copyright ©1930 by Henry Holt and Company, Inc. An excerpt of SCHOOL from *LAKE WOBEGON DAYS* by Garrison Keillor. Copyright © 1985 by Garrison Keillor. Used by permission of Viking Penguin, a division of Penguin Books USA, Inc. An excerpt from CHILDHOOD AND POETRY by Pablo Neruda from *NERUDA AND VALLEJO: SELECTED POEMS*, Beacon Press, Boston, copyright © 1976 by Robert Bly, reprinted by his permission. FROLIC reprinted with the permission of Simon & Schuster from *THE GOLDEN TREASURY*. Copyright © 1928, 1929 by the Macmillan Publishing Company. An excerpt from STILLMEADOW ROAD by Gladys Taber. Copyright © 1962 by Gladys Taber, renewed © 1990 by Constance Taber Colby. Reprinted by permission of Brandt & Brandt Literary Agents, Inc. DESK by Marina Tsvetayeva. Copyright © Oxford University Press 1971 and Elaine Feinstein 1981. Reproduced by permission of the author c/o Rogers, Coleridge & White Ltd., 20 Powis Mews, London W11 1JN. Our sincere thanks to the following authors whom we were unable to contact: Margaret E. Bruner for THE MONK AND THE PEASANT, Marie Hunter Dawson for TO AN HEIRLOOM TEAPOT, Sudie S. Hager for FRIENDSHIP, Daniel W Hickey for AUTUMN PASTORAL, Gerda Mayer for HER FRIEND FLO, and Bertha Gerneaux Woods for YELLOW FLOWERS.

How Dear to Me the Hour

How dear to me the hour when daylight dies
And sunbeams melt along the silent sea;
For then sweet dreams of other days arise
And memory breathes her vesper sigh to thee.

And as I watch the line of light that plays
Along the smooth wave tow'rd the burning west,
I long to tread that golden path of rays
And think 'twould lead to some bright isle of rest.

Thomas Moore

threads
SELECTS

7 SCRUMPTIOUS HATS TO KNIT
BABY BEANIES

DEBBY WARE